Finding Your Way

Meditations, Thoughts, and Wisdom for Living an Authentic Life

Finding Your Way

Meditations, Thoughts, and Wisdom
for Living an Authentic Life

SHARON SALZBERG

WORKMAN PUBLISHING
NEW YORK

Copyright © 2023 by Sharon Salzberg
Illustrations copyright © by Stephanie Singleton

Library of Congress Cataloging-in-Publication Data is available.

ISBN 978-1-5235-1639-1
Design by Sarah Smith

Workman books are available at special discounts when purchased in
bulk for premiums and sales promotions as well as for fundraising or
educational use. Special editions or book excerpts can also be created to
specification. For details, please contact special.markets@hbgusa.com.

Workman Publishing Co., Inc.,
a subsidiary of Hachette Book Group, Inc.
1290 Avenue of the Americas
New York, NY 10104
workman.com

WORKMAN is a registered trademark of Workman Publishing Co., Inc.,
a subsidiary of Hachette Book Group, Inc.

Printed in China on responsibly sourced paper.
First printing September 2023

10 9 8 7 6 5 4 3 2 1

*This book is dedicated to everyone
on a path to true happiness.*

Transforming in the Here and Now

In the fifty years I've been involved in practicing and teaching meditation, I have met thousands of people looking for encouragement to help navigate the daily challenges of life and remind them that they are resilient and capable. So many of us long for insight that can be easily translated into the situations of our day-to-day lives. This book offers guidance in bite-size amounts, ready to access when we need inspiration most. Each of the items is a standalone piece: a reflection to help you shift perspective, an immediate practice, an encouragement to help broaden your view and open your heart, a way to find rest for a bit, or a prompt to expand mindfulness and deepen compassion. Each emphasizes transformation in the here and now, harnessing the power of wisdom, and living the very best life we can through strengthening, caring, and connection.

The selections come in seven different shapes and sizes arrayed throughout the book, so opening to any page can offer a fresh thought, story, or suggestion.

I've included statements from my personal learning over the many years of my meditation practice that I feel are worth remembering, including during recent and particularly difficult times. The short essays offer a thought for the day or a reflection that can help change your perspective or guide you to dare to be different. You'll find snippets from compelling interviews I've had with inspiring people. I'll show a bit of what they said and why it matters. I keep a collection of arresting or inspiring quotes or passages from people I admire, and I've shared many of them here. We all need help and reminders sometimes, so you'll find one-page meditation practices on a particular theme, such as offering lovingkindness, and receiving lovingkindness offered to you. I've offered several examples of what I call *meditation in action*. That's when you combine a brief meditation practice with an activity that occurs in the midst of daily life, such as washing dishes. And I've included brief stories that illustrate a theme or the depiction of a place or a special object that has opened my heart or lifted my spirits. I think of these as soul stories.

May these pockets of inspiration, drawn from years of practice and friendship, help you as much in your life as they have in mine.

Enjoy!

Do the good in front of you, even if it feels small.

Love Is Always Present

The light of love is always in us, no matter how cold the flame. It is always present, waiting for the spark to ignite, waiting for the heart to awaken.

—bell hooks

It certainly might not feel like the light of love is always within us. Sometimes we might feel resentful of our friends and family, or get angry at ourselves, and think we have no goodness or kindness available. But all of us are born with the capacity to love and connect, and we can develop these capacities and awaken our hearts to be available no matter what the circumstances.

Overcoming Adversity

P sychologists talk about a phenomenon called Early Life Adversity. It refers to the conditions that can arise from losing parents, physical or sexual abuse, or physical or emotional neglect. I'm sure we've all at one time or another—in childhood or adulthood—felt the sting of feeling unloved, and the way it can seep into us so that we come to feel actually unlovable. I think about how likely that would be for many of the nearly half a million children in foster care in the United States.

Children in foster care who make it to adulthood often face many difficulties.

Studies have shown an increased incidence of early mortality and elevated levels of depression, suicide, and cardiovascular disease. Early life adversity can carry long-lasting ripple effects, and one of the ways that shows up is in a higher incidence of inflammation in the body—which puts a person at risk for many negative outcomes.

I was encouraged when I learned that a kind of compassion training developed at Emory University in Atlanta showed positive results in a population of children from age 13 to 17 in foster care. These young people learned, as the study reports, "to challenge unexamined assumptions regarding feelings and actions toward others, with a focus on generating spontaneous empathy and compassion for the self as well as others."

And, as a number of other studies have shown, it turns out that this friendliness and love is good for not only the metaphorical heart but for the body itself and, in the case of the Emory study, the actual physical beating heart. The researchers included biological measures (e.g., saliva tests, stress hormones) to assess whether the practice was making a difference. The children who trained themselves to generate more compassion for themselves and others showed lower levels of inflammation, and therefore may have decreased the chances of bad health outcomes in the future.

I found this an inspiring lesson for us all on the significance of challenging unexamined assumptions, like "I am not worth much" or "I can't make a difference for anyone else." When we can look at these thoughts with compassion, something truly powerful can occur: an experience of love that isn't dependent on the circumstances we find ourselves in, and that doesn't evaporate in the midst of really big challenges.

The Courage to Open to Equanimity

This is from a conversation with Joél Leon (formerly Joel L. Daniels). He is a performer, author, and storyteller, specializing in leading conversations about race, masculinity, mental health, creativity, and the performing arts. He's the author of *A Book About Things I Will Tell My Daughter* and *God Wears Durags, Too*.

JOÉL: I've found that we're made up of so many different things, and it's easy to start focusing on the things we despise most about ourselves or the things that we think "need the most work" as opposed to just being able to hold all those things. It takes courage to be with them all but not cling to them—to allow everything to fully live in that space. I can see the despair, pain, and angst, but I also know that there's something outside that's joyous, and I can hold space for both of those things. The joy doesn't take away from the despair.

We begin to see that people get to be more than one thing, situations can be more than one thing, a breath is more than one thing. In a moment, being with my own breath is a small act of courage. Seeing the breath come in with everything that's here, and seeing the breath go out and letting everything go. Asking myself: How can I give you grace? How can I offer you peace?

Those are great acts of courage that we can give ourselves on a daily basis.

And it's hard to show up in the world as ourselves because of what people may say. But the way I see it, we're all poems. I think we all have a poem in us. The less judgmental we are about how our poems manifest themselves in the world, the more truthful and joyful we are and our art is. The more we're just allowing ourselves to be liberated and detached from the way we're "supposed to" show up, the more loving and connected we become to all of ourselves.

SHARON: Even after meditating for fifty years, I've found that troublesome emotional issues don't just disappear, but rather I have an opportunity to relate differently to everything I'm going through. A friend sent me a mug emblazoned with a phrase I use often: "We feel what we feel." The reason I say that a lot is because it's been an important lesson for me. I've seen we have to allow the dignity of every feeling, without blaming ourselves or trying to push away anything. But we also don't need to take every feeling to heart, identifying with it, and imagining it is all we will ever feel. We can be with painful feelings differently, with compassion for ourselves instead of judgment. We can practice to not forget or overlook the joy and goodness that are also there. The wisdom of equanimity reminds us that we don't have to get over how we're feeling. It takes courage to turn toward ourselves with compassion and tenderly hold both our fear and joy. Somehow, we have space for both to be true because they both *are* true.

Returning to Ourselves

Take a moment to mentally step away from the pressure, the chaos, and the demands that may be surrounding you, and center your attention within yourself. Coming back to ourselves, we come back to our values, we come back to what we most deeply care about, and we can then return to action in a wiser, more balanced way.

* Stop and follow your breath for a few moments as you wait for the microwave to ding as you're heating up your lunch or the teakettle to whistle as it hits boiling.

* Before replying to a text that may provoke a reaction, take three mindful breaths and consider what you'd truly like to convey.

* Put a free minute on the calendar before every meeting for a short, follow-the-breath break.

* When you get into your car, take a moment to slow down; feel your body touching the seat before you buckle in and start the engine.

* If you pass a bench, take a moment to stop and sit for a mental breather.

* As you ease into bed, take a moment to appreciate the opportunity you have to get some rest.

The key to our deepest happiness lies in changing our vision of where to find it.

Blossoming Potential

The hidden secret of fall: the leaves
don't actually "turn" colors. With the
winter season coming, and the process
of photosynthesis being without the key
ingredients of warmth and sunshine, trees
begin to break down chlorophyll. With
the "green" gone, the other colors that
have been there all along—the magical
reds, golds, and oranges—begin to express
themselves.

—Omid Safi

This offers a resonant metaphor of a life where we all have the potential for greater wisdom, connection, love. The opportunity to realize this can never be destroyed, no matter what we have gone through, no matter what we might yet go through. That capacity might be covered over, obscured from our view, hard to discover, or hard to trust, but it is there. Given the right conditions—like our developing more awareness and self-compassion—this potential for greater wisdom, connection, and love can burst forth and begin to express itself.

Perfectionism

For me, I see a cherry pie hot from the oven as an image of perfection. The shape is perfectly round with the artful lattice crust. There is a perfect moment to eat it, when it is warm enough to melt the ice cream but not so cool that the cherries are less fragrant. Yet you are marring that perfection when you cut into the pie, even if you cut a perfectly proportioned slice. At every moment we interact, the sense of "perfection" is changing. A multitude of perfects arrives moment by moment and transitions from perfect to imperfect whether or not we're observing them. To deny the truth of change, to hold on to the "perfect," is delusion, or perfectionism.

Similarly, there is perfect love and there is perfectionism, which is a barrier to love.

Perfectionism is a brittle state focused on achieving and maintaining unwavering external standards. This is a life that is always under threat and focused on avoiding failure. When we're consumed by perfectionism, we have a negative orientation; and love for the self cannot be a refuge, because love has become too conditional, too much based on measuring performance. The illusion that supports perfectionism is the notion that, with superior self-control, we can sustain a perfect life. But one lapse and we're not perfect anymore, and our sense of ourselves plummets, taking love with it.

Real love is not about distinct objects presenting their perfections to each other. There is perfection in the connection to our shared vulnerability, not in a perfect life that guards against having any vulnerabilities at all. Through lovingkindness, compassion, and forgiveness, we can learn to accept and love our flawed and imperfect selves.

Of course, we are not perfect, but we are enough and we are complete in this moment just as we are.

Feeling Overwhelmed?

Getting more centered, even for a few moments, can help us settle into our own body and mind and not be so overcome by the agitation, or pressure, or chaos that may be happening around us.

* Use doorways as a way to focus your attention on where you are. As you come to that in-between space, feel your feet against the floor. This can bring you right into the present moment and help ground you.

* Before beginning work, set an intention for the day. For example, "May I treat everyone today with respect, whether I agree with them or not, whether I like them or not. I want to end the day free of regrets about how I speak to others." This will give you a sense of purpose no matter what is happening.

* Take a few minutes of quiet, and move your attention from seeing, to hearing, to the sensation of touch in your body. This is a way of getting centered, and it's especially helpful in providing moments of respite in a time of chaos or growing anxiety.

Moment by moment, we can find our way through.

Own Your Story

> To me, having the courage to tell your own story goes hand in hand with having the curiosity and humility to listen to others' stories.
>
> —Sarah Kay

Even if others don't consciously intend to harm us, if they are telling the story of who we are instead of our telling it, their careless disregard or easy assumptions about us can be demeaning.

We are all too often told we are too old, too young, too different, too much the same. Each of us can probably recall being misunderstood, overlooked, seemingly filed away under some category. To reclaim our own story is to reclaim our own bigger, more vibrant, more expansive potential, which no one can take away from us. When we feel confidence in our ability to live our own story, we have less to hide. This opens the door to taking a genuine interest in others, to want to more truly see them.

The *Other* Is *Us*

The tendency to regard people as "other"—as categorically different from ourselves—extends also to places and things: They are not ours; they are alien to us. But when we take a little time to be with ourselves nonjudgmentally, just seeing what we see, hearing what we hear, feeling what we feel, we get more in touch with being in our body, and we come to feel how connected we are to others: that we are the others and the others are us.

When Anurag Gupta was growing up in Delhi, his grade school teacher taught him about "other people," calling them "the ones who are not like us," the ones who are bad. When he moved to the United States at the age of ten, he suddenly became the other.

People constantly asked him, "What are you?" or "Who are you?"

When he simply answered, "I'm Anu," it did not suffice. They wanted to fit him into a box, a preexisting category of "other" that could give them a simple label to go by, which he was not interested in providing. "I knew that, from a scientific perspective, we're all *Homo sapiens*. Color is just one of the hundreds and millions of things that make us who we are as individuals."

Despite what he knew to be true, though, being confronted with the question of what he was always made him feel "separate from, other than, different from" those around him. Because he felt wounded, Anu felt "very much out of my body. I lived in my head, creating a lot of judgments." When he began a yoga practice, he found that it grounded him. "Regardless of whatever the stories, the mythologies, the biases out there about what my body is supposed to be—its color, size, background—I was at least able to experience real embodiment."

Through experiencing grounding and embodiment, he was eventually able to leave aside his stories, biases, and mythologies about others and discover a genuine sense of universal connection.

Anu went on to make it his life's work to help others transcend othering by founding BE MORE with Anu, a social enterprise that helps groups of people "measurably achieve their diversity, equity, and inclusion goals through data-driven trainings," using the raw facts of life to help us see the truth of our interconnection.

Anu is teaching what his grade school teacher overlooked: how to advance equity and belonging in your community.

Lovingkindness
for Oneself

I n a lovingkindness meditation, we can repeat phrases
expressive of the happiness we wish for ourselves. Not just
for today, but in an enduring way. Phrases that are big, that
are open. We can use the traditional phrases: *"May I be safe, may I
be happy, may I be healthy, may I live with ease of heart."* You can use
these or others that are meaningful to you; but settle on the same
few phrases, so you don't have to spend your session thinking
about them.

In this way we can connect to the love and the compassion
that exist in the world. You can imagine yourself sitting in the
center of a circle, the circle being made up of the most lovable
beings you've met, or perhaps you've never met them, but you've
been inspired by them. Maybe they exist now, or they've existed
historically or even mythically. That's the circle. And there you are,
in the center of it. It's like a circle of love just for you. Experience
yourself as the recipient of all the energy, attention, care, and
regard of all of these beings. Center your attention on repeating
three or four lovingkindness phrases as you experience yourself in
the center of that circle.

All kinds of different emotions may arise. You may feel
gratitude and awe. You might feel kind of shy, like you'd just as
soon duck down and let them give lovingkindness to one another

and forget about you. Whatever emotion may arise, you can just let it pass through you. Your touchstones are your phrases: *"May I be safe, may I be happy, may I be healthy, may I live with ease of heart."*

Imagine your skin is porous and this energy is coming in. Imagine yourself just receiving.

There's nothing special you need to do to deserve this kind of acknowledgment or care. You deserve it simply because you exist. *"May I be happy, may I be healthy..."* And you can allow that quality of lovingkindness and compassion and care to flow right back out toward that circle, and then toward all beings everywhere, so whatever you receive you transform into giving the care and kindness that does exist in this world. Then, it can become part of you and part of what you express in return.

We feel what we feel. We need to allow every feeling the dignity of its existence. Then we can decide if we want to take it to heart or let it go.

Some Things Just Hurt

Some say that if only we had a positive attitude, if only we approached our circumstances in an upbeat way, we would feel no emotional pain.

I challenge this. It's inevitable that by simply living a life, being a human being, we will encounter times of adversity. It's not because of our attitude that a pandemic or 9/11 or a financial crisis or a marriage or a long friendship ending are oppressive or heartbreaking. Some things just hurt. I have found this basic truth liberating. When I first encountered the Buddha's revolutionary statement that there is suffering in the world—in an Asian philosophy class in college—I felt instantly comforted. In fact, the comfort was unlike anything I'd experienced before.

In the teachings and practices I studied, there was no attempt to belittle my pain or rationalize it, and no one was reassuring me that things would surely get better soon or reminding me to only look at the bright side—all things we are conditioned to say and believe in the face of suffering. For the first time, I felt permission and freedom to feel whatever I was going to feel. I wasn't doing it wrong, and neither are you.

Of course, we don't want to let our suffering, and the suffering intrinsic to being a human being, define and overtake us either. Therein lies our work. So how do we do it?

For a start, it helps to recognize that for many of us, a dominant cultural attitude toward pain is that it's something to be avoided, denied, "treated." As a result, it can be particularly tough for people—including me—to acknowledge painful emotions. Simply recognizing and accepting suffering is a huge first step.

Second, remember that this truth, that some things just hurt, is universal. That means that no matter what, we are not alone.

When I'm in some kind of pain, I've found that one of the worst components of what I experience is feeling that I'm all alone with my pain, my nose pressed up against the window, looking into the space where everyone else has gathered, to enjoy themselves together or comfort one another. I'm somehow excluded, unaccounted for, and no one even notices I'm outside. It's the worst and most habitual "add-on" to suffering that I experience. And I've been experiencing it since my childhood.

But it is not actually true that we're excluded, uniquely cast out because of the pain. Everyone hurts at times. Try reaching out to someone, or allowing someone to reach out to you. Take one small step to allow whatever helping hands are coming toward you to find you.

Doing Better

I have a friend who often comments, "Everyone is just doing the best that they can." Each time, something in me rebels a bit—*Surely this person can get it together to behave better.* Or—*Surely I can get it together to behave better. Grrrr.* Then I read this quotation:

> "Do the best you can until you know better. Then when you know better, do better."
>
> —Maya Angelou

The popular and abridged form of this quotation is "When you know better, you do better," which was how I first heard it. Even with the distortion, it settled something inside of me. I know falling into the prevailing delusion about where happiness is actually to be found—perhaps in endless accumulation, perhaps in besting everyone, perhaps in never letting myself be vulnerable—leads to disconnection and confusion in my life, and I'm sure I'm not alone. This kind of disconnection and confusion creates the path to all kinds of damaging actions as we objectify and discount others rather than recognize ourselves in them. But we have the capacity to learn, to see how our lives are intertwined, how we are part of a whole. And then we can "do better"—to others and to ourselves.

We may not be able to change the circumstances of our lives, but we can change our relationship to those circumstances.

The Myth of Control

As much as we may think we do, or we should, we simply do not orchestrate all the grand motions of the universe. On a good day, we have a measure of control over ourselves—what we choose and how we behave—but beyond that, our powers are sadly limited. The awareness of a bigger picture of causes and conditions can ease our habitual, scorching self-blame for inevitable mistakes and disappointments.

Once, when I was in New York City to attend a lecture by the Vietnamese Zen teacher Thich Nhat Hanh, I was trying to hail a cab. It was the hour of the shift change, when cabdrivers will take you only if your destination matches where they need to return their cab to by an appointed hour. A driver agreed to take me uptown, but before too long, we were stuck in horrible traffic. It was like nothing I'd ever seen before. The driver tried different routes, but it was the same everywhere. I began to apologize as I feared he'd be late to return his taxi (not to mention how late I'd be for the lecture). "I am so sorry. You were nice enough to pick me up, and now you'll be late. I can't believe this traffic! I'm so, so sorry!" He interrupted me. "Madam, traffic is not your fault." He paused a moment, then said, "Nor is it mine."

I loved that he added "nor is it mine." It was such a true and wonderful teaching that I realized it might be okay if I missed Thich Nhat Hanh because I'd had an enlightened cabdriver. (I did make it, though, by about a second.)

Three Ways to Practice Lovingkindness Toward Others

W e can offer lovingkindness to various people in our lives. Start with one person and see if you can bring an image of them to mind, or feel their presence as though they were sitting right in front of you. Say their name to yourself, and offer the phrases of lovingkindness to them, focusing on just one phrase at a time. The phrases that work best are ones that are meaningful to us, phrases that convey what we would ultimately wish for all of life. The traditional phrases are:

> may you be safe
> may you be happy
> may you be healthy
> may you live with ease of heart

Gather all of your attention to say each phrase—or even just one phrase. Don't struggle to manufacture a feeling. Just relax deeply. Let the power of intention, which is the practice of lovingkindness, lead the way. When you find your attention has wandered, simply begin again. Here are examples of how to offer lovingkindness to people in various roles in our lives.

For benefactors and friends

Consider someone who has been of help to you. This person is known as a benefactor, maybe it's someone who's been directly generous to you, or kind to you, or maybe they've inspired you, even though you've never met them. In the Buddhist texts, it is said the benefactor is the one who makes us smile when we think of them.

Sit comfortably, relax. Close your eyes if you feel comfortable doing that. Get an image of your benefactor, say their name, and begin to offer the phrases of lovingkindness to them: "May you be safe, may you be happy, may you be healthy, may you live with ease of heart."

You can also practice offering lovingkindness to a friend. You can start with a friend who's doing well right now. They're enjoying success or good fortune in some aspect of life. You can get an image of them, say their name to yourself, and offer the phrases of lovingkindness to them: "May you be safe, may you be happy, may you be healthy, may you live with ease of heart."

And then a friend who's having difficulty, experiencing some kind of loss, or pain, or fear. Bring them to mind. Get a feeling for their presence, as though they were right in front of you, and offer the phrases of lovingkindness to them. Notice the different flavors of lovingkindness with these different people.

For a near-stranger

A neutral person is someone we don't strongly like or dislike. It's not an imaginary person, though. It's someone we actually encounter. They are near at hand, yet we don't know them well. Maybe it's somebody we just met, maybe it's somebody who plays a certain role in our lives, a checkout person in the supermarket, a bank teller, dry cleaner, the kind of person we tend to look right through without recognizing. Here, too, is someone who wants to be happy just as we do, who deserves to be happy.

If someone like that comes to mind, you can visualize them—you may not know their name, but you can a get a feeling for them—and then offer the phrases of lovingkindness to them: "May you be safe, may you be happy, may you be healthy, may you live with ease of heart." Notice how you feel in terms of expansiveness or openness.

For all beings

We can offer the phrases of lovingkindness to all beings everywhere, without distinction, without exception, without separation. This is an expression of our capacity to connect to and care for all of life. We begin with repetition of the phrases, "May all beings be safe. May all beings be happy. May all beings be healthy. May all beings live with ease of heart." We offer lovingkindness to all beings, then all creatures, all individuals, all those in existence. Each way of phrasing the immensity of life opens us in a slightly different way. We connect to the boundlessness of life, to so many life-forms.

We offer lovingkindness to all beings, all creatures, all those in existence stretching infinitely in front of us without boundary. Then to either side.

We offer lovingkindness to all beings, all forms of life behind us.

Then those above, and those below. "May all beings everywhere be safe, be happy, be healthy, live with ease of heart."

And when you feel ready you can open your eyes. Notice if the sense of lovingkindness affects you throughout the day.

We can go further by periodically stopping and resting.

The Anthropause

In addition to everything else it did, the arrival of COVID-19 quieted the world down for many of us. Lots of people weren't rushing around as much, there were fewer vehicles on the road, and many workplaces became silent, eliminating a lot of human-generated noise.

The way our lives receded was such a profound change that scientists could measure it. Sensors distributed around the world to listen for earthquakes charted a drop in noise of up to 50 percent in three months. This decrease was so dramatic, scientists named it the *anthropause*, or human pause.

Reading about this, I considered how this reflected mindfulness meditation, the cultivation of awareness that perceives a clearer picture of our experience. During the anthropause, sensors could hear murmurs from way down deep below the surface of the earth, signals of subtle fluctuations that are the first stirrings of bigger movements to come. During mindful meditation, what are we practicing if not distinguishing the way-down-deep signals from the everyday noise?

To meditate, we settle the body, calm the mind, and allow our senses to open so they can perceive more than just the noise given off by being caught in distractions. In a state of stillness, we may sense what is going on below our surface. In moments of meditation, when I achieve my anthropause, what I sense now, more than ever, is the depth of my connection to the world.

Before the virus hit, there were so many people we may have taken for granted as we went about our lives: taxi drivers; cleaning crews; the young man we see at the dry cleaner; and especially the healthcare workers, whose lives distinctly did *not* slow down. The virus gave us an opportunity to see how the slightest touch—how we pass by each other as we go about our lives—is a spark of connection that is both strength and vulnerability. We are in an invisible network, with each action rippling outward. Everything we do affects more than just us.

During the anthropause, we had more time to know and listen to ourselves and to see and listen to each other. When we experience fear, we often contract; but if we can pause, we can consider the world differently. We can see how a crisis has the potential to expand our vision and pull us out of our habitual characterizations. Then we can notice the things we barely saw before, especially, I hope, our deep and enduring connection to everyone around us.

Drop by Drop

I have found a simple image from one of my teachers hugely helpful: "The mind will get filled with qualities like mindfulness or lovingkindness moment by moment—just the way a bucket gets filled with water drop by drop." As soon as that image appeared in my mind's eye, I clearly saw two powerful tendencies. One was to stand by the bucket lost in fantasy about how utterly exciting and wonderful it would be when the bucket was filled, and while lost in the glories of my someday enlightenment, I am neglecting to add the next drop. The other tendency, equally strong, was to stand by the bucket in despair at how empty it was and how much more there was to go—once again not having the patience, humility, and good sense to add one drop exactly in that moment.

Because I've used the image in my teaching, I've heard variations on my own fantasies. Often people come to me and say, "I tend to completely overlook my own bucket to peer into someone else's to see how well they're doing. Is theirs fuller than mine? Is it emptier? What's going on over there?"

Comparison is disempowering. It disassociates us from our own potential.

Often people say, "I think my bucket has a leak." My response: "These buckets don't leak."

Mindfulness or lovingkindness are not objects we can either have or not have. We can never lose them. We may lose touch with these qualities of heart, but right here and now we can recover them. It is each moment of recovery that adds a drop to the bucket. In every single moment, regardless of what is happening, we can be mindful, we can be compassionate. In an instant, the mind can touch these qualities again, come to know them again. In that sense, the bucket is completely full with every drop.

Belonging

From a conversation with Sebene Selassie, meditation teacher and author of *You Belong: A Call for Connection*.

SHARON: I perceive—and I really would love your view on this—a certain quality of self-love that emerges in people when they are rising up and speaking their truth. I interviewed many social activists and change agents for my book *Real Change* and I saw that pattern: that people were having to come to a place of peace and resolve, because sometimes they got very little external support for their actions, including sometimes even from their families, who suggested that maybe they shouldn't rock the boat and just take what's offered by circumstances. But there was something in them that said, "I deserve better because all people deserve better." There is a spark of self-love at the heart of those who care for others.

SEBENE: Yeah, that's so beautiful. And we see it with the greatest social movements and the greatest social leaders: they're really grounded in love—whether it's Dr. King or Mandela or Desmond Tutu, these leaders who are coming from a place of that deep sense of belonging, of knowing their inherent worth, to rise up against systems that are constantly and often violently denying them that sense of worth. So it's true, there has to be that radical self-love in order to rise up against strong messages and forces that are trying to deny that.

SHARON: One of the most corrosive feelings any of us can have is a sense of helplessness and hopelessness. There is an interesting connection between our sense of belonging in a group and a sense of agency or ability to effect change. Do you find in your experience that belonging is kind of a prerequisite for community engagement or activism?

SEBENE: Yes. I think it's a prerequisite for any kind of social engagement and harmony, really, because if we are coming from a sense of separation, then we're in delusion. We're not seeing the truth of reality. And I say throughout my book that although we're not one, we're not separate; and although we're not separate, we're not the same.

So we have to be able to understand that paradox. The deepest and most ancient indigenous wisdom tells us that we are interconnected, and physics and science in general tell us that as well. Yet, obviously, I'm sitting here in Brooklyn; you're in Barre, Massachusetts, so we have separate relative realities, too.

To lean too much into one or the other causes a sense of dissonance and shakiness in our belonging. We can cling to the superficial harmony of "we're all one and I don't see race and we're all interconnected." Conversely, we can cling to the divisions and the challenges and the messiness that anyone who's done any amount of community or group work—especially in a multicultural context—can attest to. Belonging requires us to not lose sight of either side: We are interconnected, we're not separate, and we also have the challenges that come from our differences.

Attention is
the doorway to
compassion.

Learning to Receive Generosity

Recently, I've been thinking of how gratitude and generosity go hand in hand. Just as it is important for your spirit to be as generous as possible, it's important, when being offered generosity, to know how to accept it and to express appreciation.

The difficulty is that receiving generosity often makes people uncomfortable.

Spiritual teacher Ram Dass encountered this sticky point when he suffered a devastating stroke. He was grateful for the outpouring of gifts and support, but he admitted the hardest part was learning how to be the receiver rather than the giver. Ram Dass had been extraordinarily generous with his time and money, a natural outpouring from a man who was vigorous, bountiful, and in command of life. When life delivered a big setback, those qualities that were so much a part of him had to retreat. It was one of the many losses he faced. For Ram Dass, as for many people, when he was met with generosity from friends and strangers, he felt a sting at the comparison between his old life and the realities of the new. But eventually he commented on the fact that even though it was challenging, it was also quite liberating to receive as well as give. It was as though an internal barrier melted, and love could flow in any direction, unobstructed. All of those around him saw it in him as well, especially in the last several years of his life.

Generosity comes up against the Western ethic of valuing independence over interdependence. Many people are terrified of becoming dependent, of relying on others for support that could be withdrawn on a whim. Some feel that they don't deserve the gift or that they're not worthy of being cared for by others. They don't want to be a bother and may think that by taking something freely given, they're setting up an expectation that the gesture must be returned. The recipient may worry that they don't know if this obligation is one that they can fulfill.

My hope is that you can look through this framework: An action that increases the feeling of kindness and abundance in the world is generosity—whether small or large, whether you're on the giving or receiving end. We are all vulnerable at different times and in different ways. The boundaries around the self become more porous when you are in need. You deserve to be loved. You deserve to be cared for, and you give back when you can respond with delight and gratitude. When we receive in this way, we acknowledge the other's humanity, dignity, and goodwill. We give because we want a better world, and we do our part to make it better when we receive in that same spirit.

Praise and Blame

When we base our happiness on other people's opinion of us, we're subject to the seesaw of ambivalence, rejection, injustice, and adoration that tips this way or that depending on who likes us and who doesn't in any given moment, or on what someone else is enjoying or enduring.

When I published my first book—a dream I'd had since I was a child—I was having lunch with someone who said, "Sharon, while reading that book, I felt like I was sitting down and having a conversation with you. It's wonderful." I was awash with delight. I was so jazzed by the comment that I brought it up at dinner with friends that evening, and someone else said, "Well, that's not true. I'm reading your book and it doesn't sound like you at all. It's nothing like being with you."

I took a breath and reminded myself that you can be ecstatic at lunch and depressed at dinner—or you can take a moment and remember, it's one book! It was written from whatever was motivating me at that time, with whatever skill I could bring forth. One person took it one way, another person a different way. Of course I preferred one response over another! We are human beings—we like to be thanked, appreciated, praised. But defining ourselves by what we see in the eyes of another or requiring uniform and universal praise to be validated leads to a hollow feeling. The shifting winds of praise and blame will always exist, regardless of how skillfully—or not—we act.

We need
courage to learn
from our past
and not live in it.

True Acceptance

"I used to think healing meant ridding the body and the heart of anything that hurt. It meant putting your pain behind you, leaving it in the past. But I'm learning that's not how it works.

"Healing is figuring out how to coexist with the pain that will always live inside of you, without pretending it isn't there or allowing it to hijack your day. It is learning to confront ghosts and to carry what lingers. It is learning to embrace the people I love now instead of protecting against a future in which I am gutted by their loss."

—Suleika Jaouad, *Between Two Kingdoms*

In her book, Suleika tells the story of being diagnosed with leukemia in her twenties, going through treatment, and exploring many dimensions of healing and working with pain.

Acceptance of painful circumstances doesn't mean passivity. It means not adding shame, or a sense of isolation, or demeaning oneself while facing something difficult. That opens the door to seeking change, starting from a blossoming place of love for oneself.

At the time her book was published, Suleika had gone into remission. After that, her cancer returned, and she underwent further treatment. Her brave story shows us how acceptance is often not a one-and-done kind of thing. We call on it again and again as conditions unfold.

Kindness is
at the core of
what it means
to be alive.

Everybody Wants to Be Happy

E ven though it's a human tendency to almost exclusively remember what we've done wrong, we can consciously shift our attention to include the good within us. This is not meant to deny what's wrong or regrettable, but if we *only* think about our mistakes, we become demoralized and lose resilience. We not only lose perspective on who we actually are, we feel drained and exhausted. If we can recognize the good, we're inspired to do more of it.

Everybody wants to be happy. This is nothing to be ashamed of; it is *not* a form of selfishness. The problem is not the urge, it's ignorance—not sensing where genuine happiness might be found. The urge toward happiness itself is right and appropriate. When we can combine it with wisdom instead of ignorance, it becomes a homing instinct for freedom. This helps us cut through many obstacles.

Mindfulness is our chance to really take a look at myths we may have been taught about happiness, posing questions like:

"Does nursing that grudge make me feel stronger?" "Does compassion really bring me down?"

In so doing, we steer our lives toward genuine happiness.

The Healing Is in the Return

When you practice meditation, you can sit comfortably and relax. You don't have to feel self-conscious, as though you are about to do something special or weird. Just be at ease. It helps if your back can be straight, without being strained or arched. You can close your eyes or not, however you feel comfortable.

Notice where the feeling of the breath—just the normal flow of the in and out breath—is most predominant—at the nostrils, at the chest, or at the abdomen. Rest your attention lightly in just that area. See if you can feel just one breath, from the beginning, through the middle, to the end. If you're with the breath at the nostrils, it may be tingling, vibration, warmth, coolness. If at the abdomen, it may be movement, pressure, stretching, release. You don't have to name these sensations, but feel them. It's just one breath.

If images, sounds, emotions, or sensations arise, but they're not strong enough to actually take you away from the feeling of the breath, just let them flow on by. You don't have to follow them; you don't have to attack them. It's like seeing a friend in a crowd. You don't have to shove everyone else aside or make them go away. Regardless of what's around you, your enthusiasm and interest go toward your friend. "Oh, there's my friend. Oh, there's the breath."

When something arises—sensations, emotions, thoughts, whatever it might be—that is strong enough to take your attention away from the feeling of the breath, or if you've fallen asleep, or you get lost in some incredible fantasy, see if you can let go of the distraction and begin again, bringing your attention back to the breath. If you have to let go and begin again thousands of times, it's fine; that's the practice. The healing is in the return, not in never having wandered to begin with.

Hope

When change dawns, we want to be hopeful. Things are new, or at least we want them to feel that way. Hope can encourage us to look forward confidently.

Yet when we cling too hard to a specific outcome, our hope dips into desire, and we suffer. "Life would be perfect if I could only get that thing, person, or experience." At other times, we may feel frightened or even foolish to hope that things in our world will be better.

For some people, hopefulness feels useless, but hopelessness feels worse. What to do?

In the Buddhist tradition, we "hold hope lightly." That doesn't mean we veer toward hopelessness. In fact, it takes mindfulness to be hopeful. The opposite of hopelessness is love and connection. We move toward connection with equanimity, the wisdom born of balance. Instead of trying to wrest control over life's changes, equanimity offers us space to see the world as it is, without fixation or craving, and to see that what is in front of us is not the end of the story. It's just what we can see now.

I have found healing by remembering that things in my life have been bleak before, and that I recovered, and have even responded well to adversity. I have also found healing in a sense of community and the experience of bearing the tough times with others. Realizing we are part of a whole allows us to hold hope clearly, yet lightly.

Thoughts come up that we don't plan. We don't say, "At 9:10, I'll be filled with self-hatred." We can forgive ourselves when these painful thoughts arise, unbidden.

Am I Sluggish or Do I Really Need to Rest?

We all have times when we feel overwhelmed by the concerns of everyday life, the crises we anticipate as well as those we are experiencing right now. We slump down on the couch unable or unwilling to do anything to correct this collapse.

This could be the presence of "sloth and torpor," an ancient poetic word-pairing that describes a sluggishness or low-energy funk of mind or body, and often both, as they feed on each other. The Buddha describes the pairing as one of the five hindrances that obscure our radiant minds from seeing ourselves and the world clearly.

People hindered by sloth and torpor may be inert, but they're not relaxed. Their minds lurch from worry to sorrow and often focus on unattainable desires. Despite how much they may appear to be resting, they are exhausted.

We may begin first in developing discernment between this form of sluggishness and the body's need for rest. We all need rest, and most of us need more than we get. Rest and calm are a part of the healthy human condition. But with sloth and torpor, the amount of rest desired is out of balance with the body's requirements. When we recognize that we are indeed in an unbalanced state, how do we work with it?

A friend of mine wears a watch that she thinks of as a "sloth and torpor indicator." It's set to remind her to stand up every hour, move around, and pause to breathe. At first, she was delighted by it, but by the third day, she ripped it off her wrist and shoved it in her desk drawer, asking resentfully, "You want me to breathe now? I don't have the time."

What happens to us is not as important as the way we're relating to what is happening.

The way my friend reacted to her watch got her to ask herself some questions: Was she resentful or afraid of a commitment? Could she be kinder to herself in the face of her crankiness? It's good to be able to laugh at our annoying watch. And at our annoying minds. Laughter is a burst of energy that can restore perspective.

Our efforts begin with not making sloth and torpor our enemy. In other words, the more we add judgment, projection into the future, self-belittling, fear, hopelessness, or a sense of isolation, the more we suffer when this low-energy state comes along. If we can recognize it for what it is, without so many of those add-ons that lead us to judgment, we then have enough space to experiment with various antidotes—moving our bodies, taking a strong interest in an experience or a conversation, beginning an activity that's unfamiliar—to see if we can come into better balance.

Just Leave It in the Water

I was reminded of the healing power we have by my friend Willow. To start her New Year, Willow made a commitment to swim five times a week to help reduce her stress about her aging dad. After one particularly distracted swim, she sat down in the huge Jacuzzi next to the pool to soothe her sore muscles. There she found three people talking about the exact topic that dominated her swim. All of the others were caring for elderly relatives in various states of decline, too.

"I feel terrible about him all the time," she told her companions about her dad. "I feel like I'm doing so much and also that I'm not doing enough."

Shaking her head kindly, one of the women said to Willow (and I'm paraphrasing here), "You're doing exactly the right thing. You come here every day to heal, to try to leave your stress in the water for a while."

What Willow experienced in that moment was the buoyancy of hope, not the oppressiveness of the burden. We need to find ordinary things that can give us a break, can sustain our energy and optimism to keep us going. We do our best, live according to our values, and also acknowledge that we may not always succeed at our aspirations. Yet the actions we're taking are honorable, and those feelings of despair and inadequacy are part of the human condition. Through allowing ourselves some respite, we get perspective, we are reminded that we're part of a broader context, and we're doing the best we can with what we have. The rest we can leave in the water for a while.

To be truly happy
in this world is a
revolutionary act.

Gratitude

The things and people we are grateful for anchor us to the goodness in our lives. A moment of gratitude slices through the thicket of worries and mishaps that often grows, unchecked, in our minds.

Many of us find it easier to focus on situations that are going poorly and relationships that have become troublesome. When we're feeling low, it is especially hard to cast aside that problem-centric vision to find some peace in gratitude. In those times, gratitude requires more elbow grease and creativity.

Whenever my friend Kate needs a gratitude boost, she takes a glance at the "Favorites" list on her cell phone. There she has the people she calls most often. Next to their names are small pictures of them. Sometimes she focuses on one person, a friend from school perhaps, and is grateful for his restored health, the joy he takes in his garden, or the memory of a particular summer night on his back porch. No matter what kind of day my friend has had, she can look at her "Favorites" and remember that the good of life exists even when times are difficult.

Another friend, Susan, has developed a personal gratitude-alert setting I admire. "I have a theory that there are no ordinary things or people or places or relationships, only ordinary attention," she says. "Extraordinary attention makes ordinary things extraordinary. When I'm feeling disconnected or lonely, I do my best to remember to pay attention to details. I do my best to use my senses to take in the moment as it is happening.

"At first, I used this practice to calm my worried mind and settle my future-spinning. I then realized that paying attention—exquisite attention—is a way of falling in love. I can fall in love with the intricacies of a maple seed. I can fall in love with the sharp sounds of the blue jays and squirrels fighting nearby. I can fall in love with the poignant uncertainty of what the coming months hold. This transforms any moment from one I'm rushing through or impatient about or not noticing to one that I'm in love with. Paying attention is an investment of love in the moment."

From Me to We

> The more you understand, the more you love; the more you love, the more you understand. They are two sides of one reality. The mind of love and the mind of understanding are the same.
>
> —Thich Nhat Hanh

Practicing lovingkindness enables us to understand that the lives of all living beings are inextricably connected. As we learn to gather our attention and really listen to others, even those we've written off as not worth our time, we begin to see the humanity in people we don't know and the pain in people we find difficult.

Lovingkindness also helps us look at ourselves and others with kindness instead of reflexive criticism—to include in our concern those to whom we normally pay no attention. Focusing our attention on inclusion and caring creates powerful connections that challenge the idea of a rigid "us/them" world by offering a way to see everyone as "us."

Filling Up on Joy to Create Resilience

This is from a conversation with Jana Kiser, a social entrepreneur and founder of Global Learning, an international nonprofit dedicated to education for peace and justice.

JANA: Offering workshops in Puerto Rico after Hurricane Maria, we connected with communities through meditation, mindful movement, and music. We consciously chose to include music because like so many, I've felt how transformative the power of music can be and how much we, as humans, rely on music for joy and strength. I've found that when I take in the goodness of laughter, music, and meditation, it gives me a sense of grounding. So I look at these as paths to joy, so we have that joy as a resource to fill us up, sustain us, and allow us to keep going when things are hard.

When we practice getting in touch with a moment, either real or imagined, that gives us a sense of calm, safety, or security, we're fueling our brain with the experience of that moment. Scanning the physical space with our eyes and breathing at the same time can transform how we feel. Or focusing on a bodily sensation of safety can help our nervous systems calm down, lower our cortisol levels, and get us out of a chronic state of fight, flight, or freeze. With a sense of grounding, we have more strength and stamina to do the courageous work that is so needed to create the systemic change that our world is calling for.

SHARON: There may be times when we're trying to open to joy primarily to avoid pain, of course, but that's not always the case. When we're not motivated by denial of or aversion to pain, remembering joy can be a way of uplifting our spirit and creating resilience. When we feel depleted and burnt out, or on the edge of it, opening to joy can give us the fuel to reconnect and make a more sustained effort.

Opening to a sense of joy isn't always easy or even instinctual. According to my understanding of evolutionary biology, we're designed to look for danger, or a threat, or for what's wrong. Some say this *negativity bias* is how we're wired to survive. So it takes a kind of intentionality to also look for what's good. If we have a pleasant experience, it may pass us by, but if we're willing to pause for a moment and more completely take it in, savoring its fullness, it can give us a kind of buoyancy that allows us to see challenges differently and from a more energized, creative place.

Yin and Yang

The months and years of yin and yang are beyond measure. Although the great sages understand yin and yang, they cannot measure it. Yin and yang are all-inclusive phenomena, all-inclusive scale, and the all-inclusive way.

—Dogen Zenji

The term *all-inclusive* means nothing is excluded, and points to equanimity, which I think of these days as a heart and mind open enough to contain the immensity of life, the ability to hold seeming opposites at the same time. Joys and sorrows, the constrained present and the unknown possibilities of the future, a broken heart and the reality of love—all at the same time. It is demonstrated beautifully in the yin/yang symbol, where there is a sphere of darkness in the bright part, and a sphere of light in the dark part. In the light the darkness can be known, and in the darkness the light is always also implicit. Everything is included and beyond our attempts to measure things.

It is in the place between the known and the unknown that we find the essential truth.

Interconnection

We can become increasingly aware of how interconnected we actually are as people, as creatures, as residents of this planet. As alone and cut off as we sometimes may feel, the reality—the truth of our existence—is that we are all connected. You can go out and look at a tree and see it as a single, solitary entity. But there is also a way of looking at that tree and sensing the earth that has nurtured it, as well as the air, the sun, the moon, and the rainfall and everything that affects the quality of that rain. You might also sense all the people who have stewarded the plot of land the tree is growing on—perhaps going back for centuries. All these ways of looking at the tree—the relationships, influences, interactions—can be applied to thinking of your own life, too. How many people, how many encounters, how many joys, how many sorrows have brought you to this moment in time?

Who grew the food you've eaten today? Who transported it? How many creatures of the earth were involved in that food?

Who made the clothes you're wearing or built the building you're sitting in?

Who inspired your interest in meditation, or told you about their own meditation experience?

Who has helped you when you needed it?

Who has hurt you—in small or big ways—that inspired you to change something?

Who may have brought you to a place where you thought, "I've really got to find another way"? They may have helped lead you to be sitting here right now.

None of us really exist apart from another, completely independent. We are each part of a greater whole.

We Are All Young People

if you are far away from yourself, how could
you ever be close to another?

—Yung Pueblo

Diego Perez was born in Guayaquil, Ecuador, in 1988. His family moved to Boston, and as a teen he became involved in youth organizing, which was basically "teenagers teaching other teenagers how to organize themselves so they could change their schools or their city."

Learning the skill of organizing radically changed his life, but he found that something was missing, something was lacking. "I didn't have any inner tools to help me really deal with myself," he told me, "so I ended up getting lost along the way."

By the time he reached his early twenties, he was constantly searching outside for what he felt was lacking inside. Drug use consumed his life, until he hit a breaking point where his "body really could not keep going anymore." He had an episode where it felt like he was having a kind of heart attack and his life was slipping away. When he emerged from that, he says, "I was begging and willing for my life to continue, and I decided to make some pretty strong determinations to stop the drug abuse and start getting to know myself. For about a year, I practiced radical honesty with myself, just trying to see why I was avoiding my emotions, why I had become so addicted to pleasure. I started eating better and working out and just doing the things that my body was begging me to do."

Eventually, he heard from a friend who was traveling through India that he had attended a meditation intensive following the teachings of S. N. Goenka (the first teacher I meditated with on my first trip to India). The friend wrote a group email that talked about love, compassion, and goodwill. It shocked Diego. "I'd known him for years as a very close friend and had never heard him utter these kinds of words. All I knew was whatever happened to him, I needed some of that, too."

Inspired by his friend, he traveled to Washington state to attend a Goenka retreat. "I'd been hearing about the Buddha my whole life," he told me, "but I'd never quite resonated with the teaching and wasn't particularly interested in meditation, but hearing the word *vipassana* [insight] and encountering Goenka's exposition of the *dhamma* [Buddha's teaching] just hit so hard. I learned more in those ten days than I did in four years of college. At the end I felt so much lighter, so much freer, and it was just the very, very tip of the iceberg. I kept going back, and I started realizing that at a very deep, fundamental level, I was healing myself and that real healing was possible."

It also led him into writing in a way that would help people see themselves a little more clearly. The poet Yung Pueblo was born, which led eventually to the wildly popular book *Inward*. He chose the name Yung Pueblo because "in Guayaquil *pueblo* refers to the masses of economically impoverished people, so it reminds me of my roots, and *Yung Pueblo* literally means 'young people,' which reminds me of something I believe deeply: Humanity as a whole is very young, we have a lot of growing up to do, we are collectively still learning the simple things we're taught as children: how to be kind to one another, to tell the truth, to clean up after ourselves, to share, and not fight one another—things I'm hoping we will learn how to do well in the next hundred years."

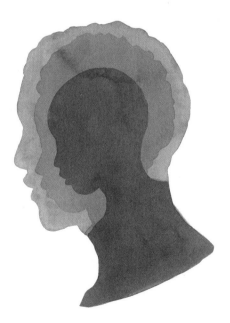

Nothing is static or fixed. The world is continually being reborn.

Open to Joy

Too much joy, I swear, is lost in our
desperation to keep it.

—Ocean Vuong

Herein lies a good deal of our day-to-day struggle and
disappointment. Something beautiful or wondrous arises,
and instead of opening to it and savoring it without reservation,
we grasp it, determined to defy the law of change and assume
control, which never works. Instead of enjoying a person or
event or object with all of our hearts for the time it is here, we've
replaced enjoyment with fearful clinging, which is a pretty bad
bargain. We can be so much happier than that.

Not Letting Our Myths Overpower Us

From a dialogue with Sona Dimidjian, PhD, director of the
Renée Crown Wellness Institute, professor of psychology
and neuroscience at the University of Colorado Boulder,
and coauthor of *Expecting Mindfully: Nourish Your Emotional
Well-Being* and *Prevent Depression During Pregnancy and
Postpartum*.

SONA: In our work, we ask participants to look closely at some of
the myths around motherhood, statements like:

> "I should be able to do all of this."
> "My job is to care for others. I can look after myself only after
> I've taken care of everyone else."
> "Asking for help is a sign of weakness."

As we look at these myths, we try to develop one of the main skills
that is a core part of mindfulness: decentering, the capacity to
notice thoughts as they arise without getting hijacked by them,
without getting sucked into them, noticing thoughts as they arise
in a space of wider awareness. For women during pregnancy or for
people in early parenting, it's often these sorts of myths that throw
people off, so we encourage them to notice those thoughts as they

arise and become curious about them, rather than automatically reacting to them.

For example, in a moment of feeling overwhelmed, the thought might arise, "Everyone else has it together. Everyone else can handle this. There's something wrong with me that I am overwhelmed in this moment." You could simply notice it within a greater field of awareness and curiosity, rather than letting the thought have the power to really knock you over.

SHARON: It's sad to see when we do this to ourselves: beat ourselves up with the myths we've inherited. And motherhood is far from the only circumstance where myths overpower us. When we consider Sona's work with mothers, though, we find another potent reminder of the power of realizing that "thoughts are not facts."

Sacred Space

fter three years in India, I returned to the United States in 1974. Joseph Goldstein, whom I had met at my first retreat in 1971, was already back, teaching at Naropa Institute's inaugural summer in Boulder, Colorado. I went to visit him there, and also met Jack Kornfield. Jack had been having a parallel life practicing meditation in Thailand while Joseph and I had been in India.

Soon after my return, Joseph, Jack, a few other friends, and I began responding to requests to lead retreats. We'd get a letter saying, "If I can gather some friends and a cook, will you come teach for ten days?" or a variation on that. Then some combination of us would make the arrangements and go teach.

In between invitations, we were largely staying in people's houses, sleeping on their living room couches or a futon on the floor with our belongings spread around. At one point a generous and frequent host said (perhaps in a quite natural wish to reclaim his living room), "I have an empty rental property in Felton, California. Why don't you go stay there for a while?"

We moved to Felton and offered the extra bedrooms in the house to people wanting to do a retreat. One of the many people to come through made a suggestion: "Why don't you start a real retreat center in this country? It can serve as a sacred site here in the United States, and the kind of energy that gets generated as people come together to meditate doesn't have to dissipate after ten days of being on retreat. I know just the people who can help you—they're all in Massachusetts."

We decided to try, and he was right—his friends in Massachusetts were crucial to the search, and the eventual opening of the Retreat Center. On February 14, 1976, we moved to Barre, Massachusetts, onto the property of what we named the Insight Meditation Society (IMS).

As the years went by, we built the Forest Refuge in the back, added various units in order to house staff, and Joseph and I built a duplex house nearby, just through the woods. Thousands of people have come to IMS to practice meditation.

I usually split my time among the center in Barre, Massachusetts; traveling; and teaching in New York City, where I have a small apartment. In March of 2020, a time I would usually spend in New York, I decided to go to Barre for what I thought would be a brief period.

Surprise! Thanks to the pandemic, I was still there months later and living a very sequestered life, given various health vulnerabilities.

In November of that year, still in Barre, I went over to the Insight Meditation Society. It had been closed to retreatants for eight months, with only a skeleton staff, practicing social distancing. I was being filmed for a teaching video and the meditation hall was the only space big enough for the camera person to be far enough away. I imagined, in returning to it after so long, I would feel a deep, chill loneliness, as though the space itself was crying out to be lived in, for someone to fill the emptiness.

I walked into the hall and was immediately struck by how it felt, filled with an intensity of light and presence and peace, as though the last meditator had left just seconds before instead of eight months prior. It was dazzling. I thought back to that comment from my friend forty-seven years ago—that a retreat center in this country could serve as a sacred site, "and the kind of energy that gets generated as people come together to meditate doesn't have to dissipate after ten days of being on retreat." I reflected, "I think you were more correct than you could have guessed." I felt so grateful for everyone who has meditated in that place, realizing how much our deeply felt effort toward awareness and good-heartedness is present in the very air we breathe.

It is the force
of love that will
lead us beyond
fragmentation,
loneliness,
and fear.

Lovingkindness

L ovingkindness has the power to change the stories we tell about ourselves: that we're alone, undeserving, or that we don't matter. It rewires these old, habitual patterns and enables us to respond in a new way. For instance, if our most ready story—the first response that shapes how we see ourselves and our world—is one of isolation, alienation, or fear, it can, with lovingkindness practice, become one of connection, caring, and kindness.

Through force of habit we can be very one-sided in our perceptions, overlooking a lot of what's positive. Maybe we criticize ourselves for not doing something perfectly, when in fact it was actually quite good enough. Or we recall how tough the afternoon was and forget the delight of the morning. Life can be so draining; a skewed view of ourselves depletes us so that we have an even harder time nourishing ourselves. Practicing lovingkindness helps us have a more balanced and compassionate view.

You can experiment with silently repeating phrases like, "May I be safe. May I be happy. May I be healthy. May I live with ease of heart."

Be Your Own BFF

Keah Brown, from her book *The Pretty One:*

> *The most amazing thing about my life now is that my own view of myself, the black disabled girl from the town no one knows the name of, has changed. I like me so much that when I think about it, I giggle like I've got a crush. When I smile it feels like the sun is filling up in my body so that when I move around the world, I can light it up. I like me so much now that I know I don't need to be the best or the prettiest person anyone meets, I just need to be me, and that's enough. The world at large is still clinging to ableist and harmful ideas of disabled people. Still, I can't allow myself to let the opinions of a culture influence my whole view the way they did before. I have too much left to do and I have worked too damn hard to get here. The rest of the world will catch up whether it wants to or not.*

The world around us may repeatedly tell us the story of who we are, but we need to craft our own narrative of who we are and what we care about and what we're capable of. Another way of saying this is that we can learn to genuinely love ourselves, with all our triumphs, all our flaws. After all, we have a life to lead as fully and authentically as we can.

Three-Minute Breathing Space

For this meditation, the first step is being aware of what is going on with you right now. Close your eyes if that feels comfortable. What thoughts are around? As best you can, just note the thoughts as events, simple discrete occurrences, in the mind. What emotions are present? Just acknowledge them, perhaps saying, "Ah, there is insecurity. Insecurity is the emotion here with me right now." And in the same way, note the sensations that are present in your body. Are there sensations of tension, of holding, of ease? Respond in the same way: "Okay, this is the sensation I'm feeling right now. This is how it is right now."

By the mere act of noticing our thoughts, sensations, and emotions as mental events, we've stepped out of automatic pilot. The second step is to collect our awareness by focusing on a single object—the movement of the breath. So gather your focus on the feeling of the in-and-out breath. It may be at the nostrils, the chest, or the abdomen. Focus on wherever it is strongest for you. Use the anchor of the breath to be present.

And now as a third step, we allow our awareness to expand to include a sense of the body *as a whole* as well as the breath. It's as if your whole body is breathing.

And then, when you are ready, just allow your eyes to open or lift your gaze.

Your heart is big enough for everyone and everything.

New Self-Talk

Whether we are facing mild travails in our lives, or dealing with more extreme times, we can address it in the same way:

Notice your emotions as they come and go—impatience, weariness, resentment, contentment. Whatever thoughts and feelings arise, try to meet them with gentle acknowledgment and kindness.

This is what's happening right now and it's okay.

In that way, we are creating an inner environment of spaciousness and lovingkindness, no matter what is happening.

The words below, which Sarah Jones, playwright and actor, posted on Instagram in December 2020, illustrate this point well. It was the ninth month of the COVID pandemic, and you may recall the prevailing collective sense of fatigue, disruption, and overwhelm so many were feeling, and how important kindness for ourselves was.

> I've been exhausted the past few weeks (months!) of all we've been walking through, politically & pandemically. I know that doesn't sound very merry, but here's the miraculous part: There's nothing wrong w/ ANY of this!! I feel messy, so tired at moments, & yet I also feel SUCH gratitude for not pathologizing myself. I'm mostly able to stay by my own side & cheer myself on in the face of all of it.

Before starting a consistent, daily self-love practice, my self-criticism was so intense, I basically spent all my time shaming & blaming myself for everything that didn't feel or look perfect (so, basically everything, since perfection is an illusion).

Now, no matter what's happening, no matter what time of year, when my head hits me w/judgment & perfectionism, a stronger voice immediately comes in to support me & remind me I'm safe, loved, & worthy. That is WILD. If you're thinking "easy for you to say," believe me, if I can get there, anyone can.

Pay Full Attention

As we jump frantically from one activity to another, we develop an aching sense of missing out on our lives. The remedy is to pay full attention, even in short interludes, many times a day. As a venerable old Tibetan lama said to me high up in the Himalayas, "Short moments, many times."

✴ Nourish yourself! Eat a meal mindfully, noticing the colors, the flavors, the texture of what you are eating.

✴ Throughout the day, experiment with walking mindfully as you go from place to place. Try not to multitask, and instead allow the walking to be a means to reset and gather yourself. Feel your feet against the ground and the sense of your body moving through space. No texting or phone calls!

✴ Unitask by focusing on just one activity for a small portion of time, settling your attention on which touch sensation is most predominant. Perhaps the feeling of your feet against the floor, or something you are holding or transporting.

Fail Forward

Don't be afraid to fail—people [are] allowed
to recover from failure and not have it be
used against them to withhold any future
they may have.

—Jonny Sun

In my experience, it appears we apply the concept of "failure" to ourselves more than anyone else. Instead, we can learn to forgive ourselves when we stumble or forget, and based on that forgiveness, reconnect to our fundamental intentions. We can utilize the understanding that everything is changing all of the time, that nothing is fixed, nothing is permanent. Because of that truth, when we make a mistake or lose sight of our aspiration, when we stray from our chosen course or don't accomplish what we had set out to do, we can respond with resilience and not hold rigidly to that idea of failure. There may be lessons to be learned, for sure, and we shouldn't ignore those, but at the same time we can emphasize recovery, starting over, and the sense of possibility.

Sometimes we need to do the best we can and then trust in the unfolding.

Rebellious Kindness

> You will learn a lot about yourself if you stretch in the direction of goodness, of bigness, of kindness, of forgiveness, of emotional bravery. Be a warrior for love.
>
> —Cheryl Strayed

I have a friend who is an independent thinker, a person who likes to set her own goals. She likes to know her varied options and tends to choose the one that is most distinctive or nonconformist, displaying her individuality. When she can be herself, and not simply fit in or try to please people, she is happy.

My friend attended a retreat some years ago, and right at the end of that intensive period of meditation she said to me, "If you really want to be a rebel, practice kindness." I loved that, and the extrapolations one could make from it: If you want to live on your own terms, breaking out from external definitions of who you are, practice love. To be free, to be bold, to be different, be kind.

A Deep Sense of Purpose

> Sometimes our journeys might seem
> uncertain and without purpose, but
> every step we take brings us closer to
> understanding why we are here.
>
> —José Andrés

I remember years ago going to eat at Jaleo, the restaurant owned by Chef Andrés in Washington, DC. It was directly across the street from my friend's apartment, where I was staying. I feel like I've watched his emergence as a humanitarian. These days I mostly hear his name in connection with the activities of World Central Kitchen, a nonprofit he founded that works in communities around the United States and the world to meet the daily needs of families in need of a warm plate of food—and supports local restaurants in the process. They have offered food to frontline medical personnel in the era of COVID and responded to those affected by devastating hurricanes in Central America, massive bushfires in Australia, fires in California, war and devastation in Ukraine and the surrounding diaspora, and in many more circumstances. Chef Andrés is a model of someone who seems to have found his deepest sense of purpose: "We're here with a simple mission, to make sure that food is an agent of change."

He encourages humanitarianism in others, by reminding us that any act of goodness, even if it seems small, like helping an elderly person place their groceries in their car, is what we need to practice. After all, his thesis is that an individual can make a difference, and there is dignity in making sure people are fed.

We are capable
of so much more
than we usually
dare to imagine.

Relatedness

Each exchange we have throughout the day, whether it's with someone we are close to or a stranger, is an opportunity to foster a sense of connection, and to bring our values of lovingkindness and compassion to life.

* For an upcoming one-on-one conversation, resolve to listen more and speak less.

* Look for ways to acknowledge someone's accomplishments.

* Look for ways to acknowledge someone's challenges.

* If you find yourself pulling away from someone, perhaps ending a conversation abruptly, lean in for a little longer.

* If someone's way of being is irritating you, try to give them the benefit of the doubt and let your judgments loosen.

* Think of someone you haven't connected with in a while, reach out, see how they're doing.

Appreciating Sound

In this meditation, we're going to spend a few minutes simply listening to sound. It can show us that we can meet any experience with greater clarity, openness, spaciousness, kindness. Even as we like certain sounds and we don't like others, we don't have to chase after them, to hold on or push away, fretfully trying to seize control over that which we will never have control over.

To begin, take a comfortable posture, eyes open or closed, and just listen. Some beautiful sounds may arise, others may be quite unpleasant or jangly. Unless you're responsible for responding to the sound, this is a time when you can practice simply being present. Noticing the sound for what it is, you don't have to elaborate, "Oh that's a bus. I wonder what the bus route is? Maybe they should change the bus route, so it's more convenient for me."

Hear the sounds that arise and pass away as though they're washing through you.

There's nothing you need to do about them, you don't need to respond, you needn't try to stop them, you don't even have to understand them. Some near, some far, some welcome, some not so welcome. Maybe it's the sound of traffic, or the wind rustling through the trees. In either case, it's simply sound arising and passing away.

Sound will emerge. You don't have to send your ears out to go and get it. Simply let yourself listen. If you find yourself getting tense in reaction to a sound, take a deep breath and let it out slowly. If you find yourself craving more of a sound, here, too you can simply relax. The sound will arise and pass away without regard to our clinging or judging. Simply notice that sound arises, we have a certain response to it, and there's a little space in between those two. And stay open for the appearance of the next sound.

The quality
of our life
depends on
our awareness.

Gratitude Is Good for Us

From a dialogue with David DeSteno, professor of psychology, Northeastern University, and author of *Emotional Success: The Power of Gratitude, Compassion, and Pride.*

DAVID: The reason we have gratitude is to shape the future, not the past. It motivates us to repay those favors—in the future—to the person who helped us, or to pay it forward to other people. So when people ask me, "Dave, I want to be a success. Should I be a nice person or a jerk—hard-driving, assertive, selfish?" I respond, "Well, what's your time frame?"

Because if you look at the evolutionary data, people who are very selfish, very hard-edged, very focused only on their own needs, can get ahead by doing that—in the short run. But over time, the ones who win are individuals who are fair and kind and generous, who show compassion, who show gratitude, because they treat people fairly and people want to continue working with them, cooperating with them, following them if they have the chance.

SHARON: That's very encouraging and relieving to hear. It could encourage those of us who feel gratitude to up the ante, to cultivate it more, paying it forward and making a better world. In Buddhist psychology, we make very fine distinctions, such as between remorse and guilt. Remorse is a forward-looking emotion—in the same way you described gratitude. It influences our behavior going forward in a positive way. By contrast, guilt simply leads to beating ourselves up with no positive effect. These fine distinctions make a difference.

Seeing the Good Within

Beginning in a relaxed, easy posture, however you feel comfortable, with eyes open or closed, see if you can think of one good thing you did yesterday. It may not have been very big or grandiose—maybe you smiled at somebody, maybe you listened to them, maybe you let go of your irritation at a slow clerk in a store, maybe you forgave yourself for not saying something totally correctly, maybe you were generous, maybe you sat down to meditate, maybe you thanked a bus driver. It's not conceit or arrogance to consider these things. It's nourishing. It replenishes the soul to take joy in the good that moves through us, that we can manifest.

And if you cannot think of something good, then the fact that you are inclining your mind toward trying is where your good lies.

Trusting Your Authentic Self

I heard a story told by writer Kent Nerburn, about when he was working as a taxi driver. I found it to be a beautiful example of authenticity in work and life.

At the end of a long shift, Nerbern got a call to pick up a customer at her home. When he arrived, he went to the door and knocked. After a long pause the door opened and an elderly woman came out "looking like someone in a movie from the 1940s" according to the driver. By her side was a small suitcase. The house looked empty. He picked up her suitcase and put it in the trunk and returned to help the woman down the steps. "She kept thanking me for my kindness. I told her it was nothing. I told her I would treat her the way I'd want my mother to be treated." When they got in the cab, she gave him the address, then asked if they could drive through downtown. It wasn't the shortest way. "I don't mind," she answered, "I'm on my way to hospice." He looked in the rearview mirror. "I don't have any family left," she said in a soft voice. "The doctor says I don't have very long." Nerbern turned off the meter and for the next two hours they drove through the city. She showed him the building where she had once worked as an elevator operator. They drove through the neighborhood where she had lived as a newlywed. Finally, the woman said she was tired and they drove to the address she had given him. After he had helped her out of the car, she asked what she owed him. He hugged her and said there was no charge. She held him tightly and said, "You gave an old woman many joyful moments. Thank you." By simply being his genuine self on the job—*by focusing on who he was on the inside as opposed to what he was expected to do for his job*—he was left with the feeling of never having done anything more important in his life.

We are
instrinsically
worthy of love.
It is not dependent
on the esteem
of others.

The Bodhi Tree in My Living Room

There is a small, potted Bodhi tree in my living room in Massachusetts. It is said the Buddha was meditating under a Bodhi tree when he became enlightened 2,600 years ago in Bodh Gaya, India. Distinguished by its heart-shaped leaves, the Bodhi tree (*Ficus religiosa*) offered the Buddha shelter through a long night of challenges—intoxicating desire, fearful visions, taunting self-doubt. Throughout it all he calmly persevered, committed to his vision of what a truly free life could look like, and as the story goes, experienced that very freedom of mind and heart with his enlightenment at the appearance of the first morning star at dawn.

After his enlightenment, it is said that the Buddha stayed in the immediate vicinity of the tree for forty-nine days, doing seven things for seven days each, so the tree remained a sanctuary for him. One of his activities was to gaze at the tree for seven days in gratitude for its having sheltered him through that long, hard night.

The tree that stands now on that spot in Bodh Gaya is said to be a direct descendant of that original tree, and it serves as a profound pilgrimage spot in the Buddhist world. When I first arrived in Bodh Gaya in December 1970, I was mesmerized by it. For one thing, it was open for people to meditate under, perform rituals under, make resolves under, reorder their lives under. You could even get permission from the caretaker to meditate under it all night; sadly (at least in my case) it yielded different results from the Buddha at dawn so long before. And truth be told, the mosquitoes and the complete absence of toilets and other amenities figured in puncturing that overly romantic dream. Nonetheless, being able to simply be there was extraordinary.

The tree in my living room grew from a cutting from the Bodhi tree in Bodh Gaya. It is too cold here to think about someday planting the tree in the ground. And besides, by the time it would become big enough for us to attempt to replant it outdoors, I'm quite confident I wouldn't be replicating the Buddha and sitting cross-legged on the ground under it. But even catching a glimpse of those leaves while I'm sitting on my living room couch brings me inspiration. I'm reminded of the Buddha's perseverance through difficulty, his commitment to not just getting by in life, his awareness that the best life can ever be is when it's filled with wisdom and compassion. I see him sitting, sheltered by that tree. Because he didn't give up, I have felt the benefit every single day of my life.

None of us exists independently. Honoring that, we can dedicate any positive energy we've generated to others—those who've helped us, and to all beings.

Acknowledgments

I am grateful to Anna Cooperberg for asking me if I'd ever considered writing a book consisting of short passages and illustrations (what I've called a gift book for years). I had not. This was March 9, 2020, a date that eventually came to be known among my friends as the last time I had lunch with someone indoors for over two years. Anna was my last pre-pandemic lunch date. A few months after the lunch I contacted Anna saying I thought it was a really good idea. I'm so glad I did.

Mary Ellen O'Neill did a remarkable job creating form and structure, layering the various elements of writing I submitted— commentary on quotations, short essays, guided meditations, edited passages from my podcast and more—plus incorporating the illustrations—to make a beautiful book in a style I'd never worked in before.

Everyone at Workman who participated in helping create the book, especially Sarah Smith, who designed the book, and Stephanie Singleton, who created the illustrations.

Joy Harris is a tremendous agent and a wonderful friend.

Barry Boyce is a greatly skilled developmental editor, talented teacher, and communicator.

And I am altogether grateful for the Insight Meditation Society and the community that has sustained it and been sustained by it for all these years. Thank you.

About the Author

S haron Salzberg is a meditation pioneer, world-renowned teacher, and *New York Times* bestselling author. She is one of the first to bring mindfulness and lovingkindness meditation to mainstream American culture more than 45 years ago, inspiring generations of meditation teachers and wellness influencers. Sharon is cofounder of the Insight Meditation Society in Barre, MA, and the author of twelve books, including the *New York Times* bestseller *Real Happiness*. Her podcast, *The Metta Hour*, has amassed five million downloads and features interviews with thought leaders from the mindfulness movement and beyond.

sharonsalzberg.com